HOW CAN I UNDERSTAND THE BIBLE?

A Way into the World's Best-seller

JOHN DRANE

BARBOUR BOOKS

An Imprint of Barbour Publishing, Inc.

Published by Barbour Books, an imprint of Barbour Publishing, Inc., P.O. Box 719, Uhrichsville, Ohio 44683
www.barbourbooks.com

ecpa Member of the
Evangelical Christian
Publishers Association

Printed in the United States of America.
5 4 3

CONTENTS

1. A World Best-seller 5

2. A Library of Books. 8

3. Ancient Manuscripts and
   Forgotten Languages 20

4. A Single Message 23

5. The Story of God's Love 27

6. Jesus at the Center 32

7. A Personal Story. 37

8. Where to Begin 40

9. Making Sense of the Bible 43

A WORLD BEST-SELLER

The Bible is without doubt the greatest classic of all world literature. Its most recent parts were written something like two thousand years ago, while the origins of its earlier sections are lost forever in the mists of time. Its story begins in the Stone Age, and ends in the world of the Roman Empire and the beginnings of the Christian church. Yet it is still the world's best-selling book.

The Bible—Facts and Figures

- In 1990, the United Bible Societies alone sold sixteen million complete Bibles worldwide—not to mention a further twelve million copies of the New Testament, twenty-seven million Bible portions, and an incredible 567 million short selections.

- When Johannes Gutenberg invented the printing press in the fifteenth century, the Bible was the first book to be printed.

- To date, the Bible has been translated into almost two thousand languages—substantially more than any other book—and has had a profound influence on the whole history of civilization.

- Wherever you travel around the world, there is a good chance that your hotel room will have a copy of the Bible.

- More than eighty percent of the world's population have access to a Bible, or a portion of it, in a language they can speak or understand.

Though its stories happened long ago and in unfamiliar places and cultures, people all over the world are still fascinated by them. Some have made extraordinary sacrifices just to have a copy of the Bible—and down through the ages, thousands have been ready to die for the privilege of being able to read it freely. Even today, millions throughout the world eagerly read it as a source of guidance and personal inspiration for daily living.

In the Bible's pages we have the rich literary treasures of two of the world's great religions: Judaism and Christianity. But religious people are not the only ones to find themselves captivated by this special book. Its unique combination of epic stories, history, reflective philosophy, poetry, political commentary—and more—has a universal appeal to all ages and all cultures. From the Stone Age to the Space Age, its power to address the needs of ordinary people has not diminished at all.

For some, however, the Bible looks rather overwhelming. So many words—it's difficult to know where to start. Others are suspicious of it, having heard vague claims that science has somehow "disproved" its message. But there must be something about the Bible, something worth exploring, if millions of people have changed their lives because of it.

If you are interested in finding out what the Bible really is all about, here's an introduction to get you started.

A LIBRARY OF BOOKS

The first thing you notice when you open a Bible is that it is not just one book. Indeed, the word "Bible" comes from a Greek word that means "books." That is what it is: a whole collection of books, gathered together over a period of hundreds of years. Or, rather, two quite separate collections of books: the Old Testament and the New Testament.

The Books of the Old Testament

THE LAW:

Genesis
Exodus
Leviticus
Numbers
Deuteronomy

THE PROPHETS:
Former Prophets

Joshua
Judges
1 Samuel
2 Samuel
1 Kings
2 Kings

Latter Prophets:	Isaiah
	Jeremiah
	Ezekiel
	Hosea
	Joel
	Amos
	Obadiah
	Jonah
	Micah
	Nahum
	Habakkuk
	Zephaniah
	Haggai
	Zechariah
	Malachi
THE WRITINGS:	Psalms
	Proverbs
	Job
	Ruth
	Esther
	Song of Solomon
	Ecclesiastes
	Lamentations
	Daniel
	Ezra
	Nehemiah
	1 Chronicles
	2 Chronicles

THE OLD TESTAMENT

The thirty-nine books of the Old Testament are the archive of a nation. They record and explain the development of the Jewish people.

These books are also the sacred Scriptures of the Jewish faith—the Hebrew Bible—and were originally organized in three sections. Although the Christian Old Testament puts the books in a different order, these three categories help us to understand their purpose and meaning. They probably indicate the three stages in which the Old Testament was put together —a process which took hundreds of years, and the work of many different authors and editors.

The Law
Five books make up the section called the Law: Genesis, Exodus, Leviticus, Numbers, and Deuteronomy. The creation stories, which is where Genesis begins, explain the relationship of God to the world, how God made it, and how evil crept into it. Some of

these books, such as Leviticus and Deuteronomy, have lists of regulations covering many different circumstances in life, and the Ten Commandments appear in Exodus.

However, not all of the contents look like law in the modern sense of a legal code. The Hebrew idea of law was much wider than that. The Hebrew word for the Law, Torah, really means "guidance" or "instruction." There are many "stories" in these books, for it was through learning the lessons of history—and especially what God was doing in it—that the Jewish people discovered how they should live.

The Prophets

This section of the Hebrew Bible is so large that it is divided into two sections.

The former prophets are the books of Joshua, Judges, 1–2 Samuel, and 1–2 Kings. They describe the early history of Israel.

The latter prophets include three famous names: Isaiah, Jeremiah, and Ezekiel, and twelve other lesser known characters: Hosea, Joel, Amos, Obadiah, Jonah, Micah, Nahum, Habakkuk, Zephaniah, Haggai, Zechariah, and Malachi. The books consist of sermons and political commentaries.

This combination of history and religious sermons might seem unusual today, but by calling the history writers "prophets," the Jews made the point that their books were not just simple records of fact. They were interpretations of the events, and they showed how the meaning of the events could be applied to the present—the lessons of history.

All the prophets—former and latter— tell how God spoke to the people of Israel. God is seen at work both in events, and though the words of particular people.

The Writings

Here is found the magnificent and moving poetry of the book of Psalms, the common-sense wisdom of Proverbs, and the story of Job, which tackles the age-old question of undeserved suffering. This section also contains the stories of two national heroines, Ruth and Esther, as well as the love poems of the Song of Solomon, the down-to-earth philosophy of Ecclesiastes, and the book of Lamentations which mourns the capture of

Jerusalem in 586 B.C.

The stories and strange visions of Daniel, and more history in the books of Ezra, Nehemiah, and 1 and 2 Chronicles, complete the coverage of ancient Israel.

Key Events of the Old Testament

The outline below corresponds to the groups of Bible books listed on pages 8–9.

THE LAW
    Abraham leaves Ur and settles in Canaan
    Isaac in Canaan
    Jacob in Canaan
    Joseph brought to power in Egypt
    Jacob's family settle in Egypt
    Jacob's descendants slaves in Egypt
    Moses leads Israelites out of Egypt
    Israelites wander in Sinai Desert

THE PROPHETS
FORMER PROPHETS
    Joshua leads Israelites into promised land; Fall of Jericho
    Israel governed by Judges: Gideon, Samson and others

Samuel, first of the prophets

Saul, first king of Israel

David, king of Israel, captures Jerusalem and
makes it his capital

Solomon, king of Israel, builds temple in
Jerusalem

Division of kingdom into Northern Kingdom
(Israel) and Southern Kingdom (Judah)

Elijah and Elisha prophets in Israel

LATTER PROPHETS

Isaiah prophet in Judah

Israel defeated and dispersed by Assyria

Jeremiah prophet in Judah

Assyrian empire collapses; Rise of Babylon

Judah defeated by Nebuchadnezzar of Babylon;
Temple destroyed; National leaders taken
captive to Babylon

Jews in exile in Babylon; Ezekiel prophet in
exile

THE WRITINGS

Babylon overthrown by Persia; Cyrus of Persia
permits return of the exiles to Judah

Ezra returns to Jerusalem, rebuilds temple;
Nehemiah returns, rebuilds walls of
Jerusalem

THE NEW TESTAMENT

When we come to the New Testament, the diversity is just as staggering. These books are not the archive of a nation. Instead, they document and describe the earliest beginnings of the Christian church. They show how the religious communities that began on the fringes of the Roman Empire soon spread through all its major cities.

The Gospels

The four Gospels—Matthew, Mark, Luke, and John—each tell the story of Jesus, the founder of Christianity. They are far from being straight biography. Like the history books of the Old Testament, they present some basic facts about His life and teaching, and then apply His message to the lives of their first readers. This explains why there are four Gospels rather than just one agreed account.

As Christianity spread into different parts of the Roman Empire, the local Christians had different needs and questions. Each of the Gospels was written for a different community:

- Matthew was most used among Jewish Christians.

- Mark was written for the persecuted Christian community in Rome.

- Luke was addressed to sophisticated and well-educated Roman and Greek citizens.

- John was initially written in Palestine, then later reissued in a Greek city, perhaps Ephesus in Asia Minor.

The Acts of the Apostles

This is Luke's continuation of the story he began in his Gospel. The word apostles means "people who have been sent out," and the book begins by telling how Jesus sent His followers out to take His teaching all over the world.

As the epic unfolds, Luke relates the exciting story of how the Christian church grew from a minority sect in Palestine to become a dominant religion in the wider Roman Empire, and even in Rome itself.

The Letters of Paul

Paul is first introduced in the stories of Acts, as one of the most enterprising of the early Christian missionaries. He was a fierce opponent of Christianity until he had a remarkable spiritual experience while traveling to the city of Damascus. He became a Christian and then traveled throughout the Mediterranean lands sharing the message of Jesus. As part of this work he wrote many letters to Christian communities—answering their questions, encouraging and informing them in their beliefs, and passing on news and greetings.

Other Books

The New Testament is completed by the letters of other Christian leaders—Peter, John, James, and Jude—written to various churches; the letter to the Hebrews, a more general book on Christian themes; and Revelation, which describes mysterious visions.

The Books and Key Events of the New Testament

A.D. 0–30

- Birth of Jesus

- Augustus Emperor of Rome
- Herod the Great king of the Jews

- Gospels:
    Matthew, Mark,
    Luke, John
    (The birth of Jesus is mentioned
        only in the Gospels of Matthew
        and Luke)

A.D. 30

- Death, resurrection, and ascension of Jesus
- Pentecost: the birth of the Church

- Tiberius Emperor of Rome
- Pontius Pilate Procurator of Judea

- Acts (The story of the early Church)

A.D. **45–58**

- Paul's missionary journeys

- Letters of Paul:
    Romans
    1–2 Corinthians
    Galatians
    Ephesians
    Philippians
    Colossians
    1–2 Thessalonians
    1–2 Timothy
    Titus
    Philemon

A.D. **70**

- Jews rebel against Rome
- Romans sack Jerusalem and destroy temple

- Other books:
    1–2 Peter
    1–3 John
    James
    Jude
    Hebrews
    Revelation

A.D. **80–96**

- Persecution of Christians by Emperor Domitian

ANCIENT MANUSCRIPTS AND FORGOTTEN LANGUAGES

The Bible is often mentioned along with Shakespeare as one of the great classics of English literature. The Bible in this context usually means the Authorized or King James Version—a translation into English produced in 1611. But the Bible is not an English book at all. Nor is it even a Western book.

The authors of the Bible wrote in everyday language: Hebrew in Old Testament times, and Greek in New Testament times.

The original language of the Old Testament was Hebrew, one of a group of languages that were known as "semitic." Other languages in this family are classical Arabic and ancient Aramaic: the official language of the Persian Empire, and the language that Jesus spoke.

Like some types of modern shorthand, the written form of Hebrew originally included only consonants. People who knew the language could easily read it, putting the right vowels in the right places. The earliest existing manuscripts of the Old Testament, which date back to four hundred years before the time of Jesus, are in this form.

Eventually, however, Hebrew fell out of common use. A group of Jewish scholars known as the Masoretes devised a set of vowels, which were inserted as dots and dashes underneath the actual letters, to indicate how they felt the words should be pronounced. The copies they made of the books of the Old Testament used this system.

Nevertheless, from the earliest days onward the Jewish scribes were very meticulous about making copies and checked them very carefully indeed.

GREEK

By the time the New Testament was written, Greek was the language spoken everywhere in the Roman Empire—a legacy from the empire of Alexander the Great.

Greek was a language with a great literary tradition. Historians and philosophers had produced many outstanding books long before the time of Jesus.

But the New Testament writers weren't aiming to produce literature—they simply wanted to communicate a message. They naturally chose to write as ordinary people would write and speak in everyday life. Many discoveries of ancient letters, invoices, and reports have shown that the Greek of the New Testament was the language of the marketplace. So when modern translators choose colloquial terms, they are not somehow corrupting the text: They are actually following the example of the original writers.

TRANSLATIONS AND VERSIONS

Since the early days of Christianity, people have wanted to read the Bible in their own language. Even now, new translations are being made in different parts of the world. Bible translators work from the original languages, using the best manuscripts available.

There are a few differences between some of the ancient manuscripts, and some Bibles indicate when a word is uncertain. In other cases, translators are not quite sure what a word means. Our knowledge of the ancient world and its languages is by no means comprehensive, but new information is coming to light all the time.

However, there are more ancient manuscripts for the Bible than for any other book of comparable age. Scholars are confident that the Bible as we now have it—both Old and New Testaments—is the Bible as it was originally intended.

A SINGLE MESSAGE

Like any other library, the Bible contains many different kinds of literature. Simple accounts of historical events stand alongside amazing visions of the spiritual world. Nonbelievers rub shoulders with women and men of the most amazing faith. And the primeval stories of its first chapters contrast sharply with the complexities of life under some of the most ruthless dictators ever seen in the ancient world. From the great epic stories of heroes such as Abraham, Moses, Joshua, or David, to the more reflective books like Job or Ecclesiastes, there is something for everyone.

This is one of the Bible's great strengths: It is a good deal easier to read a book of stories than to wrestle with a book of theology. But it can also be a weakness. With so much material to choose from, it is very easy to be sidetracked and miss the essential point of the Bible's message. Yet in spite of the variety of books, all the parts are perfectly joined together by the fact that they are part of a common story and share a common inspiration.

The Bible writers were convinced that the events they recorded and commented on were not merely the results of haphazard social, economic, or political pressures. In the course of their own lives, they had come face-to-face with God. Their writing sprang out of this relationship.

More than that, the Bible writers believed that their readers could also know God. It is this that makes the Bible a deeply religious book. It declares that this world and all its affairs are not just an accidental coincidence. In times of trouble and despair, as well as in the good times, God is there. Not as a remote, unknowable divine force, but as a caring God with whom ordinary people can—and do—have personal dealings.

The Bible contains many different kinds of literature. Compare the poetic, lyrical style of the Psalmist's song of praise with Luke's report of a key event from Jesus' life on earth.

I will praise you, O LORD, with all my heart;
I will tell of all your wonders.
I will be glad and rejoice in you;
I will sing praise to your name, O Most High.

The LORD is a refuge for the oppressed,
a stronghold in times of trouble.
Those who know your name will trust in you,
for you, LORD, have never forsaken those
who seek you.

Sing praises to the LORD, enthroned in Zion;
proclaim among the nations what he has done.
For he who avenges blood remembers;
he does not ignore the cry of the afflicted.
PSALM 9: 1–2, 9–12

25

*He went to Nazareth, where he had
been brought up, and on the Sabbath
day he went into the synagogue, as was
his custom. And he stood up to read.*

*The scroll of the prophet Isaiah
was handed to him. Unrolling it, he
found the place where it is written:
"The Spirit of the Lord is on me,
because he has anointed me to preach
good news to the poor. He has sent me
to proclaim freedom for the prisoners
and recovery of sight for the blind, to
release the oppressed, to proclaim the
year of the Lord's favor." Then he
rolled up the scroll, gave it back to the
attendant and sat down. The eyes of
everyone in the synagogue were fas-
tened on him, and he began by saying
to them, "Today this scripture is ful-
filled in your hearing."*   LUKE 4:16–21

THE STORY OF GOD'S LOVE

The story of God's love for humankind begins way back in the book of Genesis. It is focused on a childless couple living in ancient Mesopotamia. Sarah and Abraham must have been looking for a spiritual meaning in life, for the story tells how they received some remarkable challenges and promises from God.

They were to pack up their bags and move off to a new and unknown distant land. In spite of their ages, they would have a child. Both promises sounded unlikely, but in due course both things happened. They became the founders of a whole nation.

As time passed, the descendants of Abraham and Sarah became entangled with the political ambitions of one of the superpowers of the day. Generations later, the people found themselves being used by the pharaoh of Egypt as a major source of slave labour for his ambitious building projects.

The promise about being a great nation

now looked decidedly unreliable—until someone else had a remarkable experience of God. This time it was Moses. Brought up with the rulers of Egypt, but actually born into a Hebrew family, he found his life dramatically changed as God reminded him of the promise and challenged him to lead his people to freedom.

And so the slaves were set free. They escaped from cruel oppression, and they got their own land. As they later reflected on these remarkable events, they saw that this was not something that they had achieved for themselves. On the contrary, they had been too weak to do anything. Their freedom was entirely the result of God's unexpected love for them.

God's actions on their behalf showed them something of what God was like:

- God had a special concern for the poor and marginalized;

- God would help the oppressed against totalitarian forces;

- God would use ordinary people, such as Moses.

They also discovered that what God had done for them should form a model for their own way of life. As they settled in their new land, these people made a special place in their society for the poor, the marginalized, the weak, and the disadvantaged.

The rest of the Old Testament story shows how easy it was for them to forget these high ideals. Because they had enjoyed God's special love, they began to think that they were somehow better than other nations. Power often became more important than love. The result was that the nation divided against itself. Six hundred years after the escape from Egypt, it disintegrated in the face of Assyrian and Babylonian invaders.

The prophets had no doubt as to the reasons: It was all due to Israel's failure to reflect God's own love and goodness in their dealings with other people. But they did not despair. They still believed that God would show immense love for their nation.

This outpouring of love would not be

only for the benefit of the nation. Right back at the beginning, God chose Abraham so that he would be "a blessing to all the nations."

After a time of exile in Babylon, the nation was allowed to return to its own land. There followed a period which the Bible does not record in detail. The story begins again when the territory, Judea, is a minor outpost of the Roman Empire, with the New Testament.

The New Testament tells how God's love again burst through in the person of Jesus. Jesus was born to an obscure family living in rural Galilee, in a village called Nazareth.

As a man, Jesus never traveled farther than a radius of about ninety-five miles from His hometown. Yet within twenty years of His death, communities of His followers had sprung up and were thriving in all the major cities of the Roman Empire.

As people reflected on His life and teaching, they discovered God in a new and personal way. They were reminded again of God's special love for all the people of this earth.

Inspired by the spirit of Jesus, they went out and established communities in which people of all classes, both sexes, and diverse races could find a new harmony and fresh meaning in life.

The picture of God that the whole Bible provides reveals a God who showed love to women and men in many different situations. This is the Bible's main story-line. In the process, it also documents many mistakes. Then, as now, there were plenty of renegade believers who used the name of God to justify all kinds of barbarous and inhumane actions. But these were exceptions. They were frequently punished for such behavior, and they should not allow us to lose sight of the loving God, who can be personally known, who stands at the heart of the Bible story.

JESUS AT THE CENTER

Whatever we think about Him, it is impossible to ignore Jesus. This one person has had a greater impact on the world than any other single figure in the whole of history. He is controversial by any standards, and holds a compelling fascination for all who come in contact with Him. He has frequently been despised. The Romans put Him on a cross, and even His own people rejected His teachings. But for many, many people He has been—and is today—a source of personal inspiration and practical guidance.

Jesus has been the subject of the world's greatest artists. Throughout history, artists and mystics have been moved to greatness merely by thinking of the life and teachings of this man Jesus. He has been acclaimed as a hero—a prophet, even—by more than one of the world's great religions.

When Jesus was born, the whole world changed its method of reckoning time, and every time we write the date we remind ourselves of that. But who was Jesus? What can we believe about Him? Was He just a good man? Or was He God? How important is He? And what relevance, if any, does His teaching have for life in today's world? The questions seem to come endlessly. But whatever we think about Jesus, we cannot avoid Him and at the same time be true to our own personal search for meaning in life.

One thing is certain: Jesus really did exist. He is mentioned not only in the Bible, but also in other literature of the day. The Jewish historian Flavius Josephus wrote about Him, as did the Jewish Talmud.

We can also be quite certain that the Gospels of the New Testament (the four Bible books written by Matthew, Mark, Luke, and John) contain an accurate enough picture of what He was really like. The earliest of them was written down very shortly after the events they describe—and all of them were completed in less than a generation, when there would be plenty of eyewitnesses around who could correct the record.

The story of Jesus' life is deceptively simple. Brought up as the son of a village carpenter, as a young man He became a wandering religious teacher and spent about three years traveling around rural Palestine, gathering followers and claiming that He had some special insight into the nature of God and the secret of a satisfying life.

In those days He was not the only teacher of this kind. His people, the Jews, had become so demoralized by the cruel oppression of the Romans that they were ready to listen to anyone who would promise them something better. Many of these teachers had an inflated impression of themselves, and some were brazen enough to claim to be the Messiah who would rescue the Jews from their enemies, and then set up God's rule on earth.

Jesus was different.

- He was reticent to make grandiose claims for Himself, and yet He spoke with a natural authority.

- He was a person of high ideals, yet He always had time for the marginalized and the oppressed.

- He set demanding standards for Himself and his followers, yet he always allowed people space to be themselves.

- He spoke of justice, yet He always affirmed and lifted up those who were inadequate.

Above all, He spoke of God and told many stories to highlight the loving character of God. Jesus had a personal relationship with God, speaking of God as a good parent, and encouraging His followers to do the same.

It is not hard to see why people were attracted to Jesus and His teaching. But no matter how persuasive a person might be, the devotion of their followers usually ends, or at least tails off, with the death of the leader. But Jesus' death mobilized His followers in a way that not only transformed their own lives, but has had a remarkable influence on the whole of world history ever since.

Jesus was crucified—nailed to a wooden cross. It was a cruel form of death used by the Romans for the lowest kinds of criminals. Many people watched Him die. Someone offered a tomb.

But according to His followers, this was

not the end but the beginning. They were convinced that after His death, Jesus returned to life again, and was present on this earth for a period of weeks.

More than that, they experienced new power for living. They attributed this to the presence of His Spirit in their lives, and were in turn convinced that Jesus was indeed the Messiah who was expected. Not just the Messiah, but God Himself. As a result, they were inspired to remarkable feats of courage and heroism in order to spread the Christian message.

The earliest Christians were not halfwits. They knew the difference between truth and error, between imagination and facts. There can be no doubt that they themselves were totally convinced that Jesus was—and is—alive, and that their own lives had found new meaning as a result.

People are not usually prepared to die for something unless they are totally convinced of its truth. From that day to this, Christians have not flinched from being crucified, thrown to the lions, burned alive, or gunned down on the steps of a cathedral.

If they are right, then Jesus is the most remarkable person to have lived, and He demands our most serious attention.

A PERSONAL STORY

The Bible is history: There is no doubt about that.

But something about the Bible makes it more compelling than other ancient writings that are available in translation today.

My own story shows its effect.

When I was in my mid-teens, my chief claim to fame was being the class trouble-maker. I was rather proud of my repertoire of tactics for creating maximum chaos at minimum risk to myself.

When a new and inexperienced teacher of religious education arrived in my school, I was well prepared to exploit his weaknesses to the full. As he stepped through the class-room door, I rose to my feet as if making my maiden speech in parliament. I informed him that neither I nor other members of the class had any time for religion, or interest in the Bible.

To my surprise, he made straight for where I was sitting, placed his hands before me on the desk, and addressed me with that curious mixture of hesitation and recklessness typical of the novice schoolteacher.

"Tell me, Drane," he said, "have you ever read the Bible?"

I went home determined to try to read enough of it to be able to ask really awkward questions next time.

I began with one of the Gospels—Mark. I was surprised to discover the whole Gospel could actually be read between school and bedtime.

Having made that discovery, I went back the next evening to read some more. Luke, as I recall.

Then Matthew, then John. Then on to Paul's letters—many of which can be read in as little as fifteen to twenty minutes.

The discovery that it was actually possible to read the Bible in a way that made sense was exciting enough. But it was more than following the storyline.

I felt that I got to know the person called Jesus. Not a Jesus in a stained glass window who was too good to be true. Not someone locked up in theology. But a Jesus who talked about things that really mattered. About what was important in life, about the way to find happiness.

That was twenty-five years ago. But what I discovered then, others are still finding out today.

A person I met recently had spent ten years of her life drifting in and out of New Age communities, taking part in all kinds of bizarre rituals in the effort to discover true meaning in life. Until someone gave her a Bible. It was actually another New Ager, who thought that since they'd looked at the teachings of many other religious leaders, it might be worthwhile to take a glance at Jesus.

It was. But not in the way he had intended. For as my friend began to read the Bible for herself, she too discovered that this ancient book had something to say that was relevant to her personal needs.

It did not answer all her questions. But it opened her eyes to something she found totally revolutionary. She was not a conventionally religious person. She knew nothing of church and had no idea how Christians pray or worship. She simply took the Bible at face value, committed what she understood of herself to what she knew of Jesus and, in her own words, "became a totally new person."

That happened in Scotland. But the same thing is happening all over the world today, and the rediscovery of the Bible and the dynamic person of Jesus who stands at its center is bringing new hope into the lives of millions of ordinary people.

WHERE TO BEGIN

Good morning, I'd like to buy a Bible.

Certainly. Which version would you like?

Version? I thought there was only one—I want the real one, of course!

I f you're not familiar with the Bible, you may be startled by the massive array of

Bibles you can choose from. They come in all shapes and sizes, and the style of language used for the text varies from archaic to downright conversational. Some are complete Bibles, others are just a New Testament. Some books with "Bible" in the title are not the Bible text itself, but a simplified retelling.

To start reading the Bible, you need a good modern translation. There is no extra merit in having a translation that was done centuries ago—in fact it's likely that you'll find it harder to understand.

Once you open it, remember that the Bible is a collection of separate books. You wouldn't go to a library and start reading from one end of the shelves to the other. You would pick out the books that especially interest you.

In the same way, you will find it helpful to begin reading the Bible books that are easiest to grasp. The New Testament is probably the easiest place to start, especially one of the four Gospels. The longest of these—Luke— only takes a couple of hours to read, and it's a logical story, coherently retold.

As you start to read other books, you will see that they are different types of writing. Some are poetry, for example. Like other types of poetry, the writer uses words to conjure up different pictures to express the meaning. You're not supposed to take every word of it absolutely literally.

The letters present their own challenge. Paul's letters were part of an ongoing correspondence between him and his readers. But we don't know exactly what they wrote to him. There are places in the letters that feel a bit like listening to one side of a telephone conversation!

At other times, especially in the Old Testament, you may find yourself surrounded by unfamiliar names of people and places. Like any history book—or even a newspaper—it may take a bit of concentration to follow what is going on and remember who's who.

At times like this, you may find it helpful to read some background books. There are a great many of these, ranging from long commentaries to short notes. They have a similar function to the features on major world events that newspapers sometimes produce: They fill in the background, and help you understand the on-the-spot reporting that makes the headlines.

MAKING SENSE OF THE BIBLE

Beautiful landscapes. . .unspoiled mountains. . . quaint villages. . .narrow roads twisting through peaceful farmland. . .

This might be the description of any rural area. Your reaction to the words will vary enormously, depending on whether or not you have to live there, whether or not you even have the chance to visit the area.

It goes to show that when you sit down to read any book, what you read interacts with what you already know and feel.

Reading the Bible is just the same: a two-way process. Readers bring something to it, as well as expecting to get something from it. Many people bring prejudices about what they think the Bible says, and can usually convince themselves of their own opinions!

But if you want to hear the Bible's message, you have to allow it to speak to you. Some open-mindedness is required, and a spiritual openness to God. The problem is, many people find that being open to the idea of God being interested in this world is threatening, and they block off that possibility. It's rather like reading a travel book, determined in advance never to go to the place described.

When reading the Bible, I like to think of three circles interacting with one another. They are circles of stories.

- One circle is the stories of the Bible

people. People like us, mostly, with similar hopes and frustrations, fears and expectations, telling stories that helped them to make sense of things. The one thing that comes out most of all is how easy it is for people to become sidetracked from their own best intentions. Then life becomes aimless and unsatisfying.

- Another circle is God's story. God's love is shown through care for the poor and marginalized in both Old and New Testaments, and most of all in Jesus. And Jesus who died and rose from the dead gives God's power, the Holy Spirit, to His followers. God's story shows that the lives of ordinary people can be changed. The mess of the past can be forgiven. They can find new meaning and direction in life.

- A final circle is my story—and yours. It is easy to see only the first two stories in the Bible—God's and other people's. It takes courage to allow your own story to be affected by what the Bible says. But the Bible stories tell us that God is involved in birth and death, marriage and work, home and family life, and cares for people in the everyday round of life.

The story of God and God's people is going to expose many of our own weaknesses. But we see that God does not evaluate a person by his success in this world. Rather, God is on the side of the poor, and the rich and famous find it more difficult than most to get into God's Kingdom.

Of course, there is such a thing as sin—the evil that seems to run deep through the fabric of our world, and in our own lives. Yet even here there is a note of hope. For unlike many today, Jesus never puts people down—He always lifts them up and values them, including those who know that they've messed things up, to whom He brings comfort, love, and the possibility of a new life.

The Bible reveals more of our own story than any other book. If we take courage and put our story alongside the Bible's story and God's story, the living God might just break into our lives. And that can give us a new understanding of all the stories.

Inspirational Library

Beautiful purse/pocket-size editions of Christian classics bound in flexible leatherette. These books make thoughtful gifts for everyone on your list, including yourself!

When I'm on My Knees   The highly popular collection of devotional thoughts on prayer, especially for women.
    Flexible Leatherette $4.97

The Bible Promise Book   Over 1,000 promises from God's Word arranged by topic. What does God promise about matters like: Anger, Illness, Jealousy, Love, Money, Old Age, and Mercy? Find out in this book!
    Flexible Leatherette $3.97

Daily Wisdom for Women   A daily devotional for women seeking biblical wisdom to apply to their lives. Scripture taken from the New American Standard Version of the Bible.
    Flexible Leatherette $4.97

My Daily Prayer Journal   Each page is dated and features a Scripture verse and ample room for you to record your thoughts, prayers, and praises. One page for each day of the year.
    Flexible Leatherette $4.97

Available wherever books are sold.
Or order from:

Barbour Publishing, Inc.
P.O. Box 719
Uhrichsville, OH 44683
http://www.barbourbooks.com

If you order by mail, add $2.00 to your order for shipping.
Prices are subject to change without notice.